Characteristics of a Godly Marriage

The Bible Teacher's Guide

Gregory Brown

BIG Publishing

I0201659

Endorsements

"Expositional, theological, and candidly practical! I highly recommend *The Bible Teacher's Guide* for anyone seeking to better understand or teach God's Word."

—Dr. Young–Gil Kim, Founding President of Handong Global University

"Helpful to both the laymen and the serious student, *The Bible Teacher's Guide,* by Dr. Greg Brown, is outstanding!"

—Dr. Neal Weaver, President of Louisiana Baptist University

"Whether you are preparing a Bible study, a sermon, or simply wanting to dive deeper into a personal study of God's Word, these will be very helpful tools."

—Eddie Byun, Author of *Justice Awakening*

"I am happy that Greg is making his insights into

God's truth available to a wider audience through these books. They bear the hallmarks of good Bible teaching: the result of rigorous Bible study and thoroughgoing application to the lives of people."

—Ajith Fernando, Teaching Director, Youth for Christ; Author of *A Call to Joy and Pain*

"The content of the series is rich. My prayer is that God will use it to help the body of Christ grow strong."

—Dr. Min Chung, Senior Pastor of Covenant Fellowship Church (Urbana, Illinois)

"*The Bible Teacher's Guide* is thorough but concise, with thought-provoking discussion questions in each section. This is a great tool for teaching God's Word."

—Dr. Steve Pettey, Dean of Louisiana Baptist Theological Seminary

"Knowing the right questions to ask and how to go about answering them is fundamental to learning in any subject matter. Greg demonstrates this convincingly."

—Dr. William Moulder, Professor of Biblical Studies at Trinity International University

"Pastor Greg is passionate about the Word of God, rigorous and thorough in his approach to the study of it... I am pleased to recommend *The Bible Teacher's Guide* to anyone who hungers for the living Word."

—Dr. JunMo Cho, Worship Leader and Recording Artist; Professor of Linguistics at Handong Global University

"I can't imagine any student of Scripture not benefiting by this work."

—Steven J. Cole, Pastor, Flagstaff Christian Fellowship, Author of the *Riches from the Word* series

Contents

Preface

> And the things you have heard me say in the presence of many witnesses entrust to reliable men who will also be qualified to teach others.
> 2 Timothy 2:15

Paul's words to Timothy still apply to us today. We need to raise up teachers who correctly handle and fearlessly teach the Word of God. It is with this hope in mind that the Bible Teacher's Guide (BTG) series has been created. The BTG series includes both expositional studies and topical studies. This guide will be useful for personal devotions, small groups, and for teachers preparing to share God's Word.

Characteristics of a Godly Marriage is an excerpt and an adaptation from the larger work BTG First Peter. It can be used as a three-week to seven-week small-group curriculum depending how the leader chooses to divide the introduction and the six characteristics. Every week, the members of the group will read a chapter or more, answer the questions, and come prepared to share in the gathering. Each member's preparation for the small group will enrich the discussion and the learning.

Another way to lead the group is for the members to read the chapter and answer the questions together during the small group and continue with the next strategy as time allows.

I pray that the Lord may richly bless your study and use it to build his kingdom.

Introduction

Wives, in the same way be submissive to your husbands so that, if any of them do not believe the word, they may be won over without words by the behavior of their wives, when they see the purity and reverence of your lives. Your beauty should not come from outward adornment, such as braided hair and the wearing of gold jewelry and fine clothes. Instead, it should be that of your inner self, the unfading beauty of a gentle and quiet spirit, which is of great worth in God's sight. For this is the way the holy women of the past who put their hope in God used to make themselves beautiful. They were submissive to their own husbands, like Sarah, who obeyed Abraham and called him her master. You are her daughters if you do what is right and do not give way to fear. Husbands, in the same way be considerate as you live with your wives, and treat them with respect as the weaker partner and as heirs with you of the gracious gift of life, so that nothing will hinder your prayers.

1 Peter 3:1–7

What are characteristics of a godly marriage? What should we be aiming for when we are looking for a wife or a husband for those who are single? Understanding what a godly marriage looks like is very important so we can prepare for it.

It is good to remember that when God made man in his image (Gen 1:27), he made a husband and wife yoked together as one flesh (2:24). This means that the marriage relationship is a model of God and specifically the Trinity. When a marriage does not function properly, it mars the image of God and it breaks down every aspect of society.

For this reason, from the very beginning of creation, the home has been under attack. Satan attacked the home by tempting Adam and Eve in the garden. He attacks the home because it destroys the image of God, and therefore, our societies become farther and farther away from God, as the family decays and erodes. The family is the foundation of society, so when the home falls, the church falls, and when the church falls, the nation falls. As we look at this text, Peter teaches us the characteristics of a godly home, focusing on the roles of both the man and the woman.

No doubt the stress of persecution happening in the Roman Empire as Peter wrote this text, led to discord and fights in the home, particularly between husband and wife. Peter aims to correct that.

Peter also attempts to correct the common scenario of how a woman should react if she was married to a husband who had not yet come to Christ. This was very important because wives in the ancient world were often viewed as property. If she became a believer when the husband was not, it was perceived as rebellion and made the home life very difficult. On the other hand, if the husband became a believer, the wife and children were expected to follow. Therefore, Peter writes specifically to women whose lives were very difficult as a result of the former scenario.

This message is important not only for married couples, but also for singles who will one day be married. Many of us have grown up with bad models of marriage. These bad models are promoted on television, in the media, and sometimes in our own home. Most Christians do not know what a proper marriage should look like, so when they get eventually married they live out the models they have seen or experienced in the home they grew up in.

Scripture calls us to a higher model which is God's original plan for the man and the woman. We learn something of God's design in 1 Peter 3:1-7. It is a powerful remedy, not only for the church, but for our society that is cracked at the foundation as a result of our homes functioning outside of God's perfect plan.

In this study, we will consider *six characteristics* of a godly marriage.

Reflection

1. What was your parents' marriage like?
2. What are some practices that hurt marriages?
3. What are some practices that enrich marriages?
4. What other questions or thoughts do you have about this section?
5. In what ways can you pray in response? Take a second to pray as the Lord leads.

In a Godly Marriage, the Wife Submits to Her Husband to Transform Him

> Wives, in the same way be submissive to your husbands so that, if any of them do not believe the word, they may be won over without words by the behavior of their wives.
> 1 Peter 3:1

In the above passage, Peter starts off with the phrase "in the same way." This is referring to the third area of submission that should be seen in the lives of believers. He previously spoke about submitting to government (1 Pet 2:13–17) and to masters (1 Pet 2:18), and now he focuses on the home.

He is particularly focusing on the woman when he says, "Wives, in the same way be submissive to your husbands." The first point is that in a godly marriage, the wife submits to the husband in order to bring transformation in him. This call to submission is a radical concept in our culture and many rebel against Christianity because of it. Even many Christians struggle with this concept. Is the man greater than the woman? If not, then why must the woman submit to the man? Many are quite bothered by this.

However, in considering the concept of authority in the home, it has nothing to do with equality. When God called these Christians to submit to the King and to masters in chapter 2, he was not teaching inequality. An employer and an employee are fully equal; however, in order for a company to function properly, there must be authority to prevent chaos. In the same way, when God made the institution of marriage, he placed authority in the home in order that it would also function well. When we look at a society, where up to 50 percent of marriages end in divorce, we can have no doubt that marriages have lost their God-given design.

The Beginning of the Problem

In fact, we see God prophetically share this problem with Adam and Even in Genesis 3. The result of sin entering the world would be disorder in marriages. Look at what he says:

> To the woman he said, "I will greatly increase your pains in childbearing; with pain you will give birth to children. Your *desire* will be for your husband, and he will rule over you" (emphasis mine).
> Genesis 3:16

When it says the woman would "desire" the husband, it actually means the woman would desire to control the husband. We see this same word used of sin with Cain in Genesis 4:7. God said, "Sin desires you but you must master it." Sin desired to control Cain, but he was called to control it. Sin resulted in the woman seeking to usurp the leadership of the man, and it also resulted in the man trying to dominate and control the woman.

We see these dynamics in many ways throughout society. In some cultures, especially fundamentalist Muslim ones, the wife is like property and the husband can divorce or beat his wife for any offense. The husband controls and dominates the wife. In other cultures, the husband is docile in the home and the wife is the leader. In addition, we see in the feminist movement a continual push for the woman to not only usurp the man in the home, but in the church and in society, regardless of God's design.

However, we should realize that this was never God's original design for the man and the woman. Let us remember that in Genesis 1, when God made man in his image, he made them male and female. He made a plurality (Gen 1:27), just as God is a plurality. "So God created man in his own image, in the image of God he created him; male and female he created them" (Gen 1:27).

Evidence in the Trinity

Paul makes the argument in 1 Corinthians 11 that women should wear a sign of submission and submit to their husbands by calling the women to look at the Trinity. He says that the wife mirrors Christ and the man mirrors God. Look at what it says in 1 Corinthians 11:3: "Now I want you to realize that the head of every man is Christ, and *the head of the woman (or translated wife) is man, and the head of Christ is God"* (emphasis mine).

When Paul is correcting the women in the church who were dishonoring their husbands by removing their head coverings, he says the head of man is Christ. In the home, the man should submit to Christ, and the woman should submit to her husband because he is the head of the wife. Finally, he says the head of Christ is God.

Do you see the analogy with the Godhead? In the same way that the man is the head of the woman, God is the head of Christ. Christ is coequal with God, but Christ submits to the will of the Father. He says, "I came to do my Father's will. I only say what my Father says." Though equal, there is submission in the Godhead. The woman's relationship with the husband is called to mirror Christ's relationship with God. When God made mankind, he made a relationship between the husband and wife that was "one" like the Trinity, coequal like the Trinity, and had authority in it just as the Trinity. Marriage reflects the Godhead.

Now we certainly recognize that this is a hard doctrine. However, we must see that it is God's established order in Scripture. He is a God of order, and so he created it in the home. We must establish our homes on God's Word and not what would seem right to us or our culture.

Christ the Restorer

Let us understand that Christ came to reestablish biblical manhood and biblical womanhood. When sin perverted the husband-and-wife relationship, the husband became either domineering or passive and the wife either became manipulative or a doormat. This was never God's plan, and therefore, Christ came to demonstrate what the marriage should look like. He demonstrates this clearly in his relationship with the church, who is his bride. Look at Ephesians 5:22–26,

> Wives, submit to your husbands as to the Lord. For the husband is the head of the wife as Christ is the head of the church, his body, of which he is the Savior. Now as the church submits to Christ, so also wives should submit to their husbands in everything. Husbands, love your wives, just as Christ loved the church and gave himself up for her to make her holy, cleansing her by the washing with water through the word.

When we see the gospel, we see what marriage should be. Instead of the husband being lethargic while Satan leads the wife into sin, he is active. He is so active that he gives his life for his wife. He serves her by washing her with the Word of God, teaching her Scripture, leading her in holiness. He makes her beautiful. And the wife submits to him as the church should submit to Christ in everything, unless her submission would cause her to disobey God.

When the world looks at the Christian marriage, they should see the gospel. The wife submits to the husband as the church submits to Christ. The husband, instead of being lethargic or oppressive, he actively caters to the spiritual needs of his wife. When the Christian home operates like this, people see the beauty of the gospel. When the home is in disorder, it mars the gospel and it mars the image of God. It draws people away from God. It draws children away from God because it distorts God's original plan.

When Eve sinned, Adam was supposed to be like Christ and die in her place. Where the first Adam failed, the second Adam, Christ, succeeds. He shows us what biblical manhood is, as he dies for his bride, the church, and purifies her through the Word. Christ came to fix broken marriages and bring them back into the original order of the Godhead.

Power of Submission

Peter espouses the doctrine of submission as he calls the wife to submit to the husband. Let us again hear the *transformative power* of this life of submission in the wife. It is so powerful it can transform the husband. Peter says a wife who is submissive does not even need words because she lives the gospel. Look at what he says:

> Wives, in the same way be submissive to your husbands so that, if any of them do not believe the word, *they may be won over without words by the behavior of their wives*, when they see the purity and reverence of your lives (emphasis mine).
> 1 Peter 3:1–2

Here Peter gives the scenario of a wife who probably got saved after she was married and the husband was still an unbeliever. This would have created great strife in the home and possibly oppression since the wife was considered almost like property. This would have made the marriage very tough and sometimes abusive. Often in marriages like this, where the husband is an unbeliever, the woman, with right intentions, would seek zealously to win the husband to Christ. She does this by preaching at him, sometimes condemning his life of sin. Peter calls the woman to not do this.

He essentially says the life of submission which was God's perfect plan for the wife is so beautiful, so saturated with the gospel, that it could save the husband without a word. A wife who was rooted in the sin nature that came from Adam would have been trying to usurp the husband's authority their whole married life, arguing with him and seeking her own way. But all of a sudden, Christ came in resulting in this great submission. It would radically speak to the husband and potentially save his life. He would see the *purity* and the *reverence* of her life, and it lead to transformation.

In fact, we have seen this throughout history. Listen to a few of these stories of the power of a submissive life. Here is a story of a Hindu woman who was converted.

> A Hindu woman was converted, chiefly by hearing the Word of God read. She suffered very much persecution from her husband. One day a missionary asked her, "When your husband is angry and persecutes you, what do you do?"
>
> She replied: "Well, sir, I cook his food better; when he complains, I sweep the floor cleaner; and when he speaks unkindly, I answer him mildly. I try, sir, to show him that when I became a Christian, I became a better wife and a better mother."
>
> The consequence of this was that, while the husband could withstand all the preaching of the missionary, he could not stand the practical preaching of his wife, and gave his heart to God with her. [1]

Here is another story that missionary George Muller told.

George Müller told of a wealthy German whose wife was a devout believer. This man was a heavy drinker, spending late nights in the tavern. She would send the servants to bed, stay up till he returned, receive him kindly, and never scold him or complain. At times she would even have to undress him and put him to bed.

One night in the tavern he said to his cronies, "I bet if we go to my house, my wife will be sitting up, waiting for me. She'll come to the door, give us a royal welcome, and even make supper for us, if I ask her."

They were skeptical at first, but decided to go along and see. Sure enough, she came to the door, received them courteously, and willingly agreed to make supper for them without the slightest trace of resentment. After serving them, she went off to her room. As soon as she had left, one of the men began to condemn the husband. "What kind of a man are you to treat such a good woman so miserably?" The accuser got up without finishing his supper and left the house. Another did the same and another till they had all departed without eating the meal.

Within a half hour, the husband became deeply convicted of his wickedness, and especially of his heartless treatment of his wife. He went to his wife's room, asked her to pray for him, repented of his sins, and surrendered to Christ. From that time on, he became a devoted disciple of the Lord Jesus. Won without a word!

George Müller advised: Don't be discouraged if you have to suffer from unconverted relatives. Perhaps very shortly the Lord may give you the desire of your heart, and answer your prayer for them. But in the meantime, seek to commend the truth, not by reproaching them on account of their behavior toward you, but by manifesting toward them the meekness, gentleness and kindness of the Lord Jesus Christ.[2]

Again, this is not just a truth for those married to an unbeliever. This is a truth for those who are married, period. The most traveled path in a marriage to changing a husband or changing a wife is arguing and nagging, but Peter says this is largely ineffective. Oftentimes, this pushes the other person farther away, instead of closer to what God desires.

Peter says it is the power of a submissive life with purity—meaning no sin—and reverence—which is respect and honor—that has the ability to change a life. This is something that husbands and wives need to get a hold of. Yes, let us speak, but more than that, let our actions speak that our wives may be won and our husbands as well.

This should change many marriages that are largely dominated by arguing with one another. A submissive life is free of sin and sinful responses; it is a life of reverence and respect that transforms.

This life of submission is transformative because it was the life of Christ. Peter has already been arguing that this practice of submission among the authorities of the world could save lives and make them glorify God on the day of visitation (1 Pet 2:12–15); now he says it can change marriages as well.

It should be added that this text should not be used for females or males to consider dating or marrying unbelievers. Scripture speaks very clearly against that. In Nehemiah, Nehemiah starts to pull the hair out of the men that had married unbelievers (Neh 13:23–27). He essentially says, "Don't you know that Solomon lost the kingdom for this very sin?" The nation of Israel was judged for this sin.

Paul says very clearly in 2 Corinthians 6:14 that we should not be unequally yoked with unbelievers. This does not refer primarily to marriage but to every intimate relationship. Intimate relationships are yoking relationships; they pull us in a certain direction. He says the Christian who does not separate from worldy relationships will give up intimacy with God and ultimately bring discipline on their lives (v. 17, 18).

When I talk to young Christians in church or on college campuses, it seems they are largely unaware of this truth. It is like they have never read the tragic story and warnings in the Bible about courting or marrying unbelievers. It essentially led to the death of Samson and the discipline of Israel on several occasions.

Reflection

1. How does the submission of the wife to her husband model the relationships within the Trinity?
2. What are your thoughts and feelings about the submission of the wife to her husband? How can this be abused?
3. What other questions or thoughts do you have about this section?
4. In what ways can you pray in response? Take a second to pray as the Lord leads.

In a Godly Marriage, the Wife Is Focused on the Internal and Not the External

> Your beauty should not come from outward adornment, such as braided hair and the wearing of gold jewelry and fine clothes. Instead, it should be that of your inner self, the unfading beauty of a gentle and quiet spirit, which is of great worth in God's sight. For this is the way the holy women of the past who put their hope in God used to make themselves beautiful.
> 1 Peter 3:3-5

In this text, Peter begins to expand on the best way to submit to the husband and reverence him. The woman might be tempted to believe that it was all about her beauty and her outward appearance. But Peter teaches that beauty is not the primary way to honor your husband.

Now it should be noted that Peter is not saying that women should not wear jewelry or fine clothes. He is actually speaking about being consumed with it. This is seen by the fact that "fine" clothes is not in the text. It's added by translators. It literally says "do not let your adornment be clothes." Is he saying the woman can't wear clothes? No, that is why the interpreters added fine clothes. He was talking about obsession with the external.

We live in a world where the woman is tempted to often be consumed with outward adorning and her physical beauty. The world system perpetuates this. One cannot watch a commercial that doesn't say you can be more beautiful or attractive if you wear this or do that or you must look like this. God hates this focus on the external because it does not reflect the image of God. We see this in the story of the choosing of David to be king. Samuel was surveying the older brothers for kingly characteristics, and noticing one of them, he said, "Surely this must be God's anointed." However, God replies in 1 Samuel 16:7,

> But the LORD said to Samuel, "Do not consider his appearance or his height, for I have rejected him. The LORD does not look at the things man looks at. Man looks at the outward appearance, but *the LORD looks at the heart*" (emphasis mine).

God essentially says, "I do not look at people the way man does. Man is consumed with the outward appearance, but I am consumed with the heart." Therefore, when Christians are consumed with the outward appearance, they are acting like the world, not like God. You were made to look like God, to think like him. There is not one child of God who is not beautiful to him. Beauty is a work of the heart.

This would rid a lot of people of their insecurities and their pride. It would close the door on the lies that Satan speaks to so many. You must be lighter, darker, tanner, skinnier, have these kind of eyes, and this kind of nose. It is a lie. Let your focus be the inward man and not the outer man. In fact, let us see how much God hates this continual focus on the outward by how he curses the women of Israel in Isaiah 3. He says this external focus all comes from pride. Look at what he says:

> The LORD says, "*The women of Zion are haughty*, walking along with outstretched necks, flirting with their eyes, tripping along with mincing steps, with ornaments jingling on their ankles. Therefore the Lord will bring sores on the heads of the women of Zion; the LORD will make their scalps bald." In that day the Lord will snatch away their finery: the bangles and headbands and crescent necklaces, the earrings and bracelets and veils, the headdresses and ankle chains and sashes, the perfume bottles and charms, the signet rings and nose rings, the fine robes and the capes and cloaks, the purses and mirrors, and the linen garments and tiaras and shawls. Instead of fragrance there will be a stench; instead of a sash, a rope; instead of well–dressed hair, baldness;

31

instead of fine clothing, sackcloth; instead of beauty, branding (emphasis mine).
Isaiah 3:16–24

God calls them "haughty," or prideful, for being totally consumed with their outward beauty. This is a form of pride which God hates. James 4:6 says, "He opposes the proud but gives grace to the humble." God was angry with this fascination by the women of Israel with their outward appearance. When a person is all about their outward appearance: their skin, their hair, and their clothes, they are people seeking to glorify themselves instead of seeking to glorify God. Because of this pride, God judged the women of Israel.

Sad to say, many of the women in the church have become like this as well. Their focus is their bodies and their appearance, instead of the inward man. They spend more time every day on their outward man—their makeup, their clothes, their hair— instead of working on their inward man. This shows their idolatry. They run around seeking plastic surgeries because of being consumed with their outside adornment. Instead of being transformed by the Word of God. They are being conformed and pressed into the mold of the world (Romans 12:2).

This should not only be applied to clothing, for when he talks about putting jewels in one's hair, this was just an ancient way of showing one's wealth. Wealthy women would often wear their hair up high with tons of jewels wrapped in it. Today, many marriages are also consumed with signs of wealth. They want to show their wealth by having the most expensive car, the most luxurious TV, and the nicest homes. Like the world, they are consumed with the external, and they want everybody to see and know what they have. A godly marriage is not like this. It is a marriage focused on God and developing the inward man to please God.

Peter says a godly wife is not like this. He says the "adornment" of this woman is the cultivation of the internal and not the external. She clothes herself like ancient godly women as seen in Sarah, who called her husband, Abraham, master. He focuses on two particular attitudes of a godly wife: *gentle* and *quiet*.

> Instead, it should be that of your inner self, the unfading beauty of a gentle and quiet spirit, which is of great worth in God's sight. 1 Peter 3:4

What does Peter mean by the two characteristics of the "gentle and quiet spirit"? How should these be demonstrated not only in the life of the woman but the life of the man?

The word translated *gentle* or *meek* means "not insistent on one's own rights," or "not pushy, not selfishly assertive," "not demanding one's own way."[3] It is the same word used in the Beatitudes in Matthew 5:5, "Blessed are the meek for they will inherit the earth." It is actually one of the hardest words to translate in the Greek. It was used of a wild horse that had been broken and now was tamed. It means "power under control." One commentator translated this beatitude as "Blessed are those who are always angry at the right time, and never angry at the wrong time."[4]

Peter pictures a woman who is in control of her emotions and her actions. Instead of blowing up over issues, she is calculative. She ponders her responses, "Is this just my opinion, or is this something God would be angry about?" This woman desires to only be angry when God is and not at other times. She bears up under hardship and is gentle in her responses. She is Christ-like, who was also described as gentle and meek in spirit (Matt 11:29).

She is also *quiet*. This also looks back at the temptation of the woman to change her husband by her incessant words and probably complaints (1 Pet 3:1). She instead restrains her words. Solomon describes a person who restrains his words as wise. Listen to what he says in Proverbs 10:19: "When words are many, sin is not absent, but he who holds his tongue is wise." This woman is cultivating the inner man, not only to be beautiful to her husband, but to be beautiful to God. She is gentle and meek-- in control of her emotions and especially her anger. She is reserved in the use of her words. This demonstrates her wisdom.

But let us hear these are traits to be practiced not only by the woman but to be practiced by the husband as well. He is meek, in control of his emotions and his anger, and practices restraint with his words.

The Christian home is not superficial, concerned with the outward appearance. They are not consumed with the external appearance in their clothes, makeup, or skin. The godly home is not consumed with showing one's wealth through the cars or houses they buy. The secular home is consumed with these things, but not the godly home.

Let it be known that this focus on the outward appearance is a major struggle for many families including Christian ones. They are consumed with "keeping up with the Joneses" in having the latest fashions, nicest homes. The number one reason for divorce is finances. A home consumed with showing one's wealth is often a home that when the money is tight, great discord develops because they have ungodly values when it comes to how to use their finances.

But not the godly home. The godly home is totally consumed with the inside. In fact, they choose not to store up riches because it protects their heart (Matt 6:19–21), for they realize where their treasure is, their heart will be also. The godly home protects their heart from worshiping things of this world by not storing up the wealth of this world because it has a tendency to steal their heart and crowd out the Word of God as Christ taught (Matt 13:22). If their treasure is clothes, cars, phones, electronics, etc., it will detract from the heart that God loves and enjoys. The godly home is all about the inside.

Reflection

1. How have you observed the woman's temptation to be consumed with the outward as demonstrated through cultural values and the media?
2. How can she protect herself from being conformed into the value system of the world?
3. How can Christian marriages protect themselves from a shallow focus on the external?
4. What other questions or thoughts do you have about this section?
5. In what ways can you pray in response? Take a second to pray as the Lord leads.

In a Godly Marriage, the Husband Knows His Wife

> Husbands, in the same way be considerate as you live with your wives, and treat them with respect as the weaker partner and as heirs with you of the gracious gift of life, so that nothing will hinder your prayers.
> 1 Peter 3:7

After talking for six verses about the wife, the last verse is about the husband. Many have wondered if Peter gave so much attention to the woman because the majority of people in these churches were actually women. It is true that women have typically been the most spiritual partners in marriages. They are typically the ones most involved in serving. As pastors, we often watch the wives from the pulpit who are intently watching and listening, while the husbands are struggling to stay awake during service.

This shows part of the reason the church, the home, and our society are in such a poor state. Not many men are willing to step up and lead like Christ in the home and in society by setting a righteous example.

There is a tremendous need to restore biblical manhood in the church, where men are assertive in leading spiritually.

I often tell my wife if I was one of the single girls on a college campus these days, most likely I would just stay single. So few men are willing to be spiritual leaders. I remember leading a Lifestyle Discipleship School one semester at the university, which started every weekday morning at 7:00 am. We had about twenty people, and only three to five of them were guys. I pulled the guys aside and said, "Look at this. This is a commentary on the church. It shows the man's spiritual lethargy." Let me tell you, we are already praying for my daughter's husband and she is only a baby. There is a tremendous lack of male spiritual leadership in the church.

With that said, this makes this one verse so important for us to hear. Even though it's only one and the ladies get six, it is a verse that is loaded, and we need to focus on it. We will actually pull several points out of this one verse. In this verse, he gives men a secret on how to love and better serve their wives. Listen again to 1 Peter 3:7: "Husbands, in the same way be considerate as you live with your wives."

"Be considerate" in the NIV is better translated "dwell with them according to knowledge," as seen in the KJV.

What is one of the things a husband must do to develop a godly marriage? He must develop a knowledge base.

What type of knowledge should the husband cultivate, and how should he cultivate it? The husband must cultivate several types of knowledge.

1. The husband must "know" *his wife.*

Let me first say it's hard to teach on the role of the husband because I fail at this in many ways. *The husband should intently study his wife*. He needs to learn her likes and her dislikes so he can better minister to her.

I will share a little about one of the things I have learned about my wife. My wife is a hard worker, and she is very empathetic with people. She cares for others. But because of this, she sometimes takes on too much of a load, whether it is meeting with people or cooking for them. I've seen this tendency manifest itself in frustration or weariness.

One of the ways I have learned to love her is by protecting her. I will say, "No, you're not cooking for small group this week. We are going to order out. You're getting worn down." Or as she is the primary caregiver for our daughter, Saiyah, sometimes if Saiyah is having a bad night, I will take care of Saiyah. Why? It's because I know my wife. If my wife doesn't get sleep, she doesn't function well. I've had to develop a knowledge base about my wife so I can better serve her. I know she really likes it if I do things around the house. Sometimes, if she's getting worn out, I'll help out more.

When we first got married, I just watched and didn't do much to help or serve her. I could see the pattern that would lead toward frustration but never really responded to it. This in turn brought frustration in the marriage. Now I am a veteran of over seven years and I have learned to better understand her rhythms and my rhythm. I do not claim to be good at this, but because I'm studying her, I'm getting better.

How else does the husband dwell with his wife according to knowledge?

2. The husband must "know" *Scripture.*

I think this is one of the things implied by this knowledge the husband must have. If he is going to be a godly husband, he must not only know his wife but Scripture as well and relate to his wife on the basis of Scripture. Listen to Ephesians 5:25–27:

> Husbands, love your wives, just as Christ loved the church and gave himself up for her to make her holy, cleansing her by the *washing with water through the word*, and to present her to himself as a radiant church, without stain or wrinkle or any other

blemish, but holy and blameless (emphasis mine).
Ephesians 5:25–27

Here in this text, the primary way the husband loves his wife is by washing her with the Word of God. One of the things the husband must do in serving his wife is study the Word of God with her, teach her the Word of God, and also help her apply it so she can be without stain or wrinkle. He needs to wash her blemishes, her insecurities. He must build her up in the inner person so she can fulfill all that God has called her to do. The husband plays the role of Christ. In the same way that Christ equips the church to serve through the Word of God, he calls the husband to equip his wife.

The husband must dwell with his wife according to the knowledge of Scripture. The husband needs to learn and study Scripture in order to be obedient to God. He may apply this knowledge by leading in family devotions, taking the family to a Bible-preaching church, and simply exhorting the wife and children to daily holiness.

This is very important for young single women to understand so that as they search for a husband, they will look for a man who is a spiritual leader. I know the pickings are slim. The world can give you a husband, but a godly spouse is a gift from the Lord. Listen to Proverbs 19:14: "Houses and wealth are inherited from parents, but a prudent wife is from the LORD." You need to wait for your gift and not compromise. Look for someone who knows the Word and teaches it not only with their mouths but with their lives.

This is also a call for young men to prepare themselves. Prepare yourself to lead a family by knowing the Word of God and being involved in serving God's church. What else is the man called to do?

Reflection

1. What are some unique things you have learned about your spouse that help you better serve him or her?
2. How can you be more faithful in serving your spouse?
3. For singles, how is God calling you to grow in your "knowledge" in order to be a godly mate?
4. What other questions or thoughts do you have about this section?
5. In what ways can you pray in response? Take a second to pray as the Lord leads.

In a Godly Marriage, the Husband Needs to Dwell with His Wife

> Husbands, in the same way be considerate *as you live* with your wives, and treat them with respect as the weaker partner and as heirs with you of the gracious gift of life, so that nothing will hinder your prayers (emphasis mine).
> 1 Peter 3:7 (ESV)

Peter says the husband must "live with" his wife as seen in the ESV. Again, it literally can be translated "dwell together with." This means that in order to be a godly husband, you must spend time with your wife and in fact *be at home*. This is very important to say because many homes fail specifically on this issue. The husband is not at home. He is not at home because of work; he is not at home because of pleasure. He is not at home because at home there is stress.

One of the things needed for a godly marriage is for the husband to dwell with his wife. Often in our society the job demands have become almost unreasonable. Satan is the ruler of this world, the ruler of this wicked age, and he knows what he is doing.

In some jobs, it is almost impossible for a husband to be at home, and that includes the pastorate. One of the reasons pastor kids and missionary kids have such bad reputations is because many times, the fathers, the pastors, are not around. They are too busy doing ministry. Look, it is impossible to be a good pastor without being a good husband and a father (1 Tim 3:2). And in order to do this, men must be at home. In fact, this is something I have seen a lot in the church since I served as a youth pastor for seven years. Listen to what Paul said in Ephesians 6:4: "Fathers, do not exasperate your children; instead, bring them up in the training and instruction of the Lord" (or "Do not provoke your children to wrath" in the KJV).

Paul tells the fathers to not push the children to wrath but to train them in the instruction of the Lord. In order to train them in the instruction of the Lord, the father has to be around. One of the main ways a child is provoked to wrath is because fathers are not home. Many of these children grow up not really knowing their father because he was never around, and therefore, they grow up with tremendous anger. *We are raising an angry generation of children.* And as you know, children whose fathers are not around are more prone to divorce, crime, abuse, depression, suicide, etc. Why? It's because they are angry.

44

Listen, in order to have a godly marriage, husbands/fathers have to be at home. You have to "dwell together with your wife." You need to be home with your kids. Now practically this may mean changing careers or having a lesser level of living. A lot of these jobs today will not let you be home. That's one of the things I have to consider when looking at ministry jobs.

Our churches are so far away from God they, in a sense, demand for pastors to not be good fathers or husbands. Not me! I want to honor God before I honor any church or job. First Timothy 5:4 and 8 says the first priority of our religion must be our family and anyone who neglects this is worse than an infidel. Even unbelievers care for their family.

A characteristic of a godly marriage is the husband being home, dwelling with his wife and kids.

Reflection

1. Do you feel that it's true that godly male leadership is in high demand but low supply?
2. How do you think godly single women should respond to this drought? What about vice versa?
3. What other questions or thoughts do you have about this section?

4. In what ways can you pray in response? Take a second to pray as the Lord leads.

In a Godly Marriage, Couples Honor Their Differences

> Husbands, in the same way be considerate as you live with your wives, and treat them with respect as the weaker partner.
> 1 Peter 3:7

Next, Peter tells the husband to treat her with respect, or better translated "honor," as the weaker partner or vessel. What does he mean by weaker vessel?

He seems to be referring to the physical strength of the woman. In general, men are stronger physically than women and also sometimes emotionally. Because he has made the woman's body to bear children, there are tremendous hormonal differences in comparison to the body of the man that sometimes affects the emotions.

The husband must honor these differences, rather than beleaguering them, which is very common in marriage. One of the ways this often plays out in marriage is that husbands and wives look upon these differences with disdain. They just don't understand one another. In one sense, the husband tries to make the woman more masculine like he is. The wife tries to make the husband more feminine.

Why does Peter tell the husbands to be more considerate about the wives and not vice versa?

I like to think of the husband's vessel being like a brick and the wife's like a delicate vase. If God calls the brick and the vase to dance, which vessel is typically going to get hurt? The vase will. Many times marriage is like this. The brick is constantly hurting the vase. They have a different structure, and therefore, the brick needs to be delicate in how he handles the vase.

This is a shallow illustration of something I've learned in marriage. I was raised to be a "man's man," or so I like to think, in part because of my athletic background. My wife and I like to banter over stuff like the milk expiration date. My wife likes to throw away the milk the day the milk is past the date. I like to go, "No babe, that is the best sold by date. It's not necessarily bad. Let's not throw out the milk."

One of the ways I've learned how to deal with this and, similar issues, is recognizing that we are just different. I want to eat the leftovers that have been in the fridge for a week, and my wife wants to throw them away. But the reality is, most things I eat I don't get sick over. My vessel is a like a brick; I'm not too concerned about getting sick from food or day-old coffee. My wife's body is different; some things that I eat she might get sick from. We are different in many ways. I've had to learn how to accept these differences, and to honor them as well.

We even see this in parenting styles. My wife is a woman and is very delicate with the baby, delicate with her eating, and of course, I am not. I was throwing Saiyah in the air the first week she was born. I was doing flips with her. I am male. We have learned to respect and honor our differences. I like to sneak Saiyah ice cream when Momma is not around.

These may be bad illustrations that show how crazy I really am, but God has given males and females different vessels, and it affects how we interact with other people and our environment. For many marriages, these differences are a source of constant conflict. We need to honor the delicateness or the strength of the other vessel. Some things that would not bother you emotionally will probably bother your mate. Males and females are different, and these differences must be honored.

It should be noted that the word *respect* in the NIV is not strong enough. Most commentators would argue for the word *honor* as in the ESV. Husbands must not only respect their wives but honor them.

What are some practical ways spouses can honor one another?

1. Listen to them.
2. Take time to enjoy the activities they enjoy. Sometimes the woman will honor the husband and their differences by enjoying certain sports or shows with him that she wouldn't normally enjoy. Maybe the husband will go shopping with the wife or watch the Home TV Network.
3. Praise them. Thank them for what they do. We need to show appreciation daily for our spouses and their differences.

Reflection

1. What types of differences commonly cause conflict between males and females, especially in marriage?
2. How have you dealt with these differences in the past?
3. What other questions or thoughts do you have about this section?
4. In what ways can you pray in response? Take a second to pray as the Lord leads.

In a Godly Marriage, Couples Experience Unhindered Powerful Prayer

> Husbands, in the same way be considerate as you live with your wives, and treat them with respect as the weaker partner and as heirs with you of the gracious gift of life, so that nothing will hinder *your* prayers (emphasis mine).
> 1 Peter 3:7

One of the things that is interesting about this text is the *your* in "hinder your prayers" is actually plural. Though some commentators believe this is referring to the husbands' prayers, many believe Peter is referring to the couples' prayers being hindered. If this is true, the implication is that the husband and wife are expected to have a corporate prayer life. They are praying individually and praying corporately. And when they are walking in unity with one another, God is answering their prayers. They pray for souls to be saved together, people to be healed, finances to come in to help people, and this godly couple is seeing answers to their prayers.

This should be what we see in the life of a godly couple all the time.

The godly couple's life of unity makes their prayers powerful. Listen to what Christ said:

> Again, I tell you that if two of you on earth agree about anything you ask for, it will be done for you by my Father in heaven. For where two or three come together in my name, there am I with them.
> Matthew 18:19–20

Christ taught that great power is in corporate prayer as people come together and agree with one another. This is one of the greatest things I have found about marriage. It has increased and strengthened my prayer life. Marriage is a powerful union, in part, because of the power of corporate prayer that comes with it. I have no doubt this is one of the reasons Satan works so hard against unity in the marriage because he knows it is a powder keg in getting God's will done on the earth.

For that reason, Peter warns that strife in a relationship actually hinders the prayers of a couple; it makes their prayers ineffective. We see this principle generally taught throughout Scripture. Listen to what David said in Psalms 66:18: "If I had cherished sin in my heart, the Lord would not have listened."

We also see specifically that living in anger with someone actually opens the door for the evil one in our lives. Look what Paul said in Ephesians 4:26–27: "'In your anger do not sin': Do not let the sun go down while you are still angry, and *do not give the devil a foothold*" (emphasis mine).

Many couples, by their disputing, not only close the door to their prayer life and make it unprofitable, but they give the devil a foothold, which is a war term. This means that the discord gives him an area to wage war on the marriage and their lives in order to bring destruction to it. Many couples live with a war going on that has been embellished by the work of the devil, and there is no help for them. God doesn't hear their prayers because they refuse to forgive one another or give grace. Therefore, the devil continues to war. Godly couples live in prayer, and God answers their prayers.

Reflection

1. Do you find your prayer life more effective by yourself or in a group of two or more? Why or why not?
2. What ways have you seen discord hinder your prayer life?
3. What other questions or thoughts do you have about this section?
4. In what ways can you pray in response? Take a second to pray as the Lord leads.

Conclusion

What are characteristics of a godly marriage?

1. In a Godly Marriage, the Wife Submits to Her Husband to Transform Him
2. In a Godly Marriage, the Wife Is Focused on the Internal and Not the External
3. In a Godly Marriage, the Husband Knows His Wife
4. In a Godly Marriage, the Husband Needs to Dwell with His Wife
5. In a Godly Marriage, Couples Honor Their Differences
6. In a Godly Marriage, Couples Experience Unhindered Powerful Prayer

Walking the Romans Road

How can a person be saved? From what is he saved? How can someone have eternal life? Scripture teaches that after death each person will spend eternity either in heaven or hell. How can a person go to heaven?

Paul said this to Timothy:

> But as for you, continue in what you have learned and have become convinced of, because you know those from whom you learned it, and how from infancy you have known the holy Scriptures, which are *able to make you wise for salvation through faith in Christ Jesus.*
> 2 Timothy 3:14-15

One of the reasons God gave us Scripture is to make us wise for salvation. This means that without it nobody can know how to be saved.

Well then, how can a people be saved and what are they being saved from? A common method of sharing the good news of salvation is through the Romans Road. One of the great themes, not only of the Bible, but specifically of the book of Romans is salvation. In Romans, the author, Paul, clearly details the steps we must take in order to be saved.

How can we be saved? What steps must we take?

Step One: We Must Accept that We Are Sinners

Romans 3:23 says, "For all have sinned and fall short of the glory of God." What does it mean to sin? The word sin means "to miss the mark." The mark we missed is looking like God. When God created mankind in the Genesis narrative, he created man in the "image of God" (1:27). The "image of God" means many things, but probably, most importantly it means we were made to be holy just as he is holy. Man was made moral. We were meant to reflect God's holiness in every way: the way we think, the way we talk, and the way we act. And any time we miss the mark in these areas, we commit sin.

Furthermore, we do not only sin when we commit a sinful act such as: lying, stealing, or cheating; again, we sin anytime we have a wrong heart motive. The greatest commandments in Scripture are to "Love God with all our heart, mind, and soul and to love others as ourselves" (Matt 22:36-40, paraphrase). Whenever we don't love God supremely and love others as ourselves, we sin and fall short of the glory of God. For this reason, man is always in a state of sinning. Sadly, even if our actions are good, our heart is bad. I have never loved God with my whole heart, mind, and soul and neither has anybody else. Therefore, we have all sinned and fall short of the glory of God (Rom 3:23). We have all missed the mark of God's holiness and we must accept this.

What's the next step?

Step Two: We Must Understand We Are under the Judgment of God

Why are we under the judgment of God? It is because of our sins. Scripture teaches God is not only a loving God, but he is a just God. And his justice requires judgment for each of our sins. Romans 6:23 says, "For the wages of sin is death."

A wage is something we earn. Every time we sin, we earn the wage of death. What is death? Death really means separation. In physical death, the body is separated from the spirit, but in spiritual death, man is separated from God. Man currently lives in a state of spiritual death (cf. Eph 2:1-3). We do not love God, obey him, or know him as we should. Therefore, man is in a state of death.

Moreover, one day at our physical death, if we have not been saved, we will spend eternity separated from God in a very real hell. In hell, we will pay the wage for each of our sins. Therefore, in hell people will experience various degrees of punishment (cf. Lk 12:47-48). This places man in a very dangerous predicament—unholy and therefore under the judgment of God.

How should we respond to this? This leads us to our third step.

Step Three: We Must Recognize God Has Invited All to Accept His Free Gift of Salvation

Romans 6:23 does not stop at the wages of sin being death. It says, "For the wages of sin is death, but the gift of God is eternal life through Jesus Christ our Lord." Because God loved everybody on the earth, he offered the free gift of eternal life, which anyone can receive through Jesus Christ.

Because it is a gift, it cannot be earned. We cannot work for it. Ephesians 2:8-9 says, "For it is by grace you have been saved, through faith—and this not from yourselves, it is the gift of God—not by works, so that no one can boast."

Going to church, being baptized, giving to the poor, or doing any other righteous work does not save. Salvation is a gift that must be received from God. It is a gift that has been prepared by his effort alone.

How do we receive this free gift?

Step Four: We Must Believe Jesus Christ Died for Our Sins and Rose from the Dead

If we are going to receive this free gift, we must believe in God's Son, Jesus Christ. Because God loved us, cared for us, and didn't want us to be separated from him eternally, he sent his Son to die for our sins. Romans 5:8 says, "But God demonstrates his own love for us in this: While we were still sinners, Christ died for us." Similarly, John 3:16 says, "For God so loved the world that he gave his only begotten son that whosoever believeth in him should not perish but have eternal life." God so loved us that he gave his only Son for our sins.

Jesus Christ was a real, historical person who lived 2,000 years ago. He was born of a virgin. He lived a perfect life. He was put to death by the Romans and the Jews. And he rose again on the third day. In his death, he took our sins and God's wrath for them and gave us his perfect righteousness so we could be accepted by God. Second Corinthians 5:21 says, "God made him who had no sin to be sin for us, so that in him we might become the righteousness of God." God did all this so we could be saved from his wrath.

Christ's death satisfied the just anger of God over our sins. When God saw Jesus on the cross, he saw us and our sins and therefore judged Jesus. And now, when God sees those who are saved, he sees his righteous Son and accepts us. In salvation, we have become the righteousness of God.

If we are going to be saved, if we are going to receive this free gift of salvation, we must believe in Christ's death, burial, and resurrection for our sins (cf. 1 Cor 15:3-5, Rom 10:9-10). Do you believe?

Step Five: We Must Confess Christ as Lord of Our Lives

Romans 10:9-10 says,

That if you confess with your mouth, "Jesus is Lord," and believe in your heart that God raised him from the dead, you will be saved. For it is with your heart that you believe and are justified, and it is with your mouth that you confess and are saved.

Not only must we believe, but we must confess Christ as Lord of our lives. It is one thing to believe in Christ but another thing to follow Christ. Simple belief does not save. Christ must be our Lord. James said this: "Even the demons believe and shudder" (James 2:19) but the demons are not saved—Christ is not their Lord.

Another aspect of making Christ Lord is *repentance*. Repentance really means a change of mind that leads to a change of direction. Before we met Christ, we were living our own life and following our own sinful desires. But when we get saved, our mind and direction change. We start to follow Christ as Lord.

How do we make this commitment to the lordship of Christ so we can be saved? Paul said we must confess with our mouth "Jesus is Lord" as we believe in him. Romans 10:13 says, "Everyone who calls on the name of the Lord will be saved."

If you admit that you are a sinner and understand you are under God's wrath because of them; if you believe Jesus Christ is the Son of God, that he died on the cross for your sins, and rose from the dead for your salvation; if you are ready to turn from your sin and cling to Christ as Lord, you can be saved.

If this is your heart, then you can pray this prayer and commit to following Christ as your Lord.

Dear heavenly Father, I confess I am a sinner and have fallen short of your glory, what you made me for. I believe Jesus Christ died on the cross to pay the penalty for my sins and rose from the dead so I can have eternal life. I am turning away from my sin and accepting you as my Lord and Savior. Come into my life and change me. Thank you for your gift of salvation.

Scripture teaches that if you truly accepted Christ as your Lord, then you are a new creation. Second Corinthians 5:17 says, "Therefore, if anyone is in Christ, he is a new creation; the old has gone, the new has come!" God has forgiven your sins (1 John 1:9), he has given you his Holy Spirit (Rom 8:15), and he is going to disciple you and make you into the image of his Son (cf. Rom 8:29). He will never leave you nor forsake you (Heb 13:5), and he will complete the work he has begun in your life (Phil 1:6). In heaven, angels and saints are rejoicing because of your commitment to Christ (Lk 15:7).

Praise God for his great salvation! May God keep you in his hand, empower you through the Holy Spirit, train you through mature believers, and use you to build his kingdom! "The one who calls you is faithful, he will do it" (1 Thess 5:24). God bless you!

Coming Soon

Praise the Lord for your interest in studying and teaching God's Word. If God has blessed you through the BTG series, please partner with us in petitioning God to greatly use this series to encourage and build his Church. Also, please consider leaving an Amazon review. By doing this, you help spread the "Word." Thanks for your partnership in the gospel from the first day until now (Phil 1:4-5).

Available:
First Peter
Theology Proper
Building Foundations for a Godly Marriage
Colossians
God's Battle Plan for Purity

Coming Soon:
Nehemiah
Philippians
Abraham
Ephesians

About the Author

Greg Brown earned his MA in religion and MA in teaching from Trinity International University, an MRE from Liberty University, and a PhD in theology from Louisiana Baptist University. He has served over ten years in pastoral ministry and currently serves as Chaplain and Assistant Professor at Handong Global University, pastor at Handong International Congregation, and as a Navy Reserve chaplain.

Greg married his lovely wife Tara Jayne in 2006, and they have one daughter, Saiyah Grace. He enjoys going on dates with his wife, playing with his daughter, reading, writing, studying in coffee shops, working out, and following the NBA and UFC. His pursuit in life, simply stated, is "to know God and to be found faithful by Him."

To connect with Greg, please follow at http://www.pgregbrown.com.

Notes

1. Teacher's Outline and Study Bible – Commentary – Teacher's Outline and Study Bible – 1 Peter

2. MacDonald, W. (1995). *Believer's Bible Commentary: Old and New Testaments* (A. Farstad, Ed.) (1 Peter 3:2). Nashville: Thomas Nelson.

3. Grudem, W. A. (1988). *Vol. 17*: *1 Peter: An introduction and commentary*. Tyndale New Testament Commentaries (148). Downers Grove, IL: InterVarsity Press.

4. Barclay, W. (2001). *The Gospel of Matthew* (Third Ed.). The New Daily Study Bible (111). Edinburgh: Saint Andrew Press.